PAPERBACK POETS 7: **r.a.simpson**

Gramley Library
Salem Academy and College
Winston-Salem, N.C. 27108

diver
r.a.simpson

UNIVERSITY OF QUEENSLAND PRESS

SALEM COLLEGE LIBRARY
WINSTON-SALEM, N. C.

PR
6037
I7135
D5

also by R.A. Simpson

The Walk Along the Beach
This Real Pompeii
After the Assassination

Published by University of Queensland
Press, St. Lucia, Queensland, 1972
© R.A. Simpson, 1972
Typed on an IBM Composer
Printed and bound by
Peninsula Press Limited, Hong Kong.
National Library of Australia card
number and ISBN 0 7022 0740 3

Distributed by International Scholarly
Book Services, Inc.
Great Britain—Europe—North America

Designed by Cyrelle

This book is copyright.
Apart from any fair dealing
for the purposes of private
study, research, criticism
or review, as permitted under
the Copyright Act, no part
may be reproduced by any
process without written
permission. Enquiries should
be made to the publishers.

for Alexander Craig

95595

Acknowledgment is made to

the *Age*
the *Australian*
Australian Poetry (Angus &
    Robertson)
Australian Poetry Now (Sun Books)
Meanjin Quarterly
Poetry Australia
Poetry Magazine
Spirit (U.S.A.)
the *Sydney Morning Herald*
Twelve Poets 1960-1970 (Jacaranda
    Press)

contents

III Hardiman's progress

I

diver

Alone on the tower
I'm not confident.
The water is black
And distant.

I think of style
And raise my arms and aim,
Holding back the plunge.
It's mostly a game

That touches terror,
Then terror goes—
I view my fingers,
My toes.

'Defiance, love and revolt
Make the diver dive
And prove, through dying,
He's alive,'
A voice preaches in my head. . .

And so I dive.

Water gulps me down,
Chilling me with its grip,
Then arms pine up and up
Like worship.

castaway

1

The fish, the birds, and gradually a coast
At first a mirage in the mist.

The island
Grew like those insights that show the self.
And then I read the lack of green, the rocks,
The loneliness from hill to hill. I knew
My days of deserts and droughts had begun.
More fish than man, I lost the grip of water.

2

My boat is languid wreckage in the shallows.
Here I must improvise.

A child again
I'll be a parent to myself
And pamper, scold and tutor for survival
Till I appear a despot or a clown
To test my wits with animals, the wood
And grass, discover means to keep this life.
My past, my present and the future
Are water vague toward the horizon—
And
The fleeting clarity of foam on sand.

friend and ocean

Six years ago on rocks—
Nimble, with lines for fish—
We talked about the bushfire,
Dante. Again the coastal morning
Lightens without complexity.

Here I believe nothing's changed.
Top-heavy waves half-moon
And turn to nothing in long lines.
I can't exhume
Much of what we said.

For you, for me,
Six years were mainly work
Not unlike the sea
Working on this beach.
Children run ahead, collecting shells:

They come to water tamed and trapped in rocks.
Here minute fish are shooting stars—
Go under shelves to hide;
But I recall the same green sky
As shallow, not as wide.

lake

I can't hold it, keep it.
It's full of mountains fluttering down,
And trees—or rather their other selves.

I can break it with a stone,
My foot; and I can almost see
Just what it's thinking. I'm certain it's thinking.

A fisherman unpacks himself gently
On a ledge, and soon his line
Is holding the lake exactly.

tunnels

I ask myself to laugh;
My laughter's like a croak.
That needle-point of light
Could be a joke.

My feet in muddy water,
My fingers reading walls,
Like fingers knowing braille,
As someone calls

In me? Out there?
The needle-point of light
Expands—the only kind
Of deity in sight—

It lords my view.
Escape.
And so I dare,
And engine like an ape

Toward another opening
That blinds with so much fire
After so much dark. Tunnels
Follow tunnels of desire.

midnight

Police sirens die
At midnight on the highway,
And winter marbles the sky.
My television dies, leaving
The look of a blind man:
Far off, a bedroom sigh

While I sit gauging
Nothing more than seraphim
Raging
In a book, warring in a cloud
Outside my room.
My mind is always staging

Fantasies, charades—but I recall,
For what reason I can't say,
A midnight, a man dying. . . his fall
Away from life alone
With me standing near his bed, watching—
That's all.

Midnight is a mirror and a wall.

find the saviour

1
a few words

What am I worth?
A few words arranged
With taste? Worth little?

Why the questions now?
The house is steady;
Money comes in weekly.

I'm in demand.
People ring me;
Children wait for me.

Sometimes I'm told
Someone likes my words:
I like being told—

And then I wake
The way I wake
On Monday morning.

Some years are left?

Desire and dread
Remain.
I'll unlock the earth.

2
often

Often I've tried to kill
Friendships, and if this sounds
Absurd I'll explain
That what I try to kill
Is being near, being revealed
Often. Desiring gifts,
I know that I don't give
Often. But I suppose
The tortoise and the platypus
(Names that just occur; others would easily do)
Are trapped by being tortoise
And platypus.

This can't be all,
Says the romanticist.
And so the feelings, doubts, go on
Often.
            Give me a look at God,
            Though I know the sky;
            I've circled its core, the moon.

3
1943

My uncle used the war
Driving a taxi;
American soldiers were easy,
Optimistic with their money.
I went to the pictures.
I'd never heard of prostitutes
Or what they did—busy
With retreats, confessions on a Friday.

There's a photograph
Showing first communicants;
I was fourteen, caught
Because my mother thought—
The teaching Brothers thought
(Perhaps I thought)
I could be good and holy
After my atheistic father died;
He was better.

I recall mornings
After my mother dreamt of races,
Horses winning, and yet she won little.
We've both learnt to write from gentle, distant places.

SALEM COLLEGE LIBRARY
WINSTON-SALEM, N. C.

4
4 a.m.

I can't sleep;
Nothing unusual.
Words don't work,
Merely heap
Themselves in the dark,
Making torment.
I'll force some mark
Upon vacuity.
I lift myself and look
Into the only deep
I really know—
Or do I know?
Through the window
There's a clothes-line,
A wet shirt in the night
(Or rather in this early morning)
Hanging like a man
Expiring, growing light.

this room only

Walking through this insubstantial room
You try to touch the walls
But find them cloud, fog or smoke.
Your feet aren't walking on real wood,
They're walking in a mist that doesn't let you sink.
Strange. The room goes on and on
And photographs of Groucho Marx are fused
To every wall, wise-cracking all the time
About being nowhere really, acceptance.
Suddenly you know that you're contained
In one enormous laugh where you must praise.

when

When the bridge began to crack, I wondered if this sewer-city was about to enter the river and become merely reflections— the banks empty of buildings apart from a few charred stumps and the rat-eyes of the Premier standing in for stars. God?

When I think of God these days, I suppose I should think of Bonhoeffer plunging, dying, bleaching—a gift of dust going nowhere forever and greeted by 'Hullo God'.

When I sense, try to know, try to love in the night, I see my pumpkin self—but despite this I learn to celebrate

When I forget and remember concurrently.

contacts with the past

1
going past

Solid and dull, my primary school
Hasn't changed its bricks,
And dunce-eyed in a car
I go past quickly;

But I'm always near
The boy who's made too clear
By words I use, the way I love:
For thirty years I've fired my air-gun at a dove.

2
aces

I saw them differently
When I was twelve;
I saw them heroically
Climbing into Sopwith Camels
And fingering their goggles.
They rose lightly,
Dissolved in cloud above Cambrai,
Softly, cunningly.
The tragic and absurd
Photographs of 1918 flyers
Have lost their innocence,
And days dissolve in me.

3

the drawing

My drawing of Brother Coghlan
Went secretly around the class.
Fourteen, in my shell,
I turned to glass

When he looked right down at me.
During Latin he lined
All forty boys around the room:
For years he had refined

His timing with the strap .
Few boys forgot a word.
The Apostles stared: the dove
Appeared the cruellest bird.

Today I found the drawing
Deep in a box. I wonder
What he hated. Each smile he coined,
Attempt at kindness, became a blunder.

revisiting Adelaide

1

Before I left that year
I walked the garden of a house
Where my parents planted a bush
Aeons ago.
I pillaged some leaves and left
Them in my pocket to rot.

Today mountains perish into clouds
That mountain even higher above this city,
And offer themselves as souvenirs.

2

Now
on this
shore I put
this cairn for yet
one more gentleman
whose failures surround him—

then turn it upside-down
because mountains
aren't memories,
deserve such
treatment
now.

birthday

This is my birthday.
I'm told,
'Life begins at forty.'
I'm neither young nor old.

Off-stage I tell myself
To resurrect my life:
The framework's truly shaky.
My children and my wife

Accept Aquarius;
They've made a cake,
And candles burn strictly
For celebration's sake.

I'm asked to blow them out:
My breath, remarkably, is true.
I look for auguries
In most things that I do.

the bug

My son likes it,
This golden bug,
And puts it in a match-box.

It's perfectly dead.
He stabs it with a pin,
A test for pain.

He feels the thrust himself,
But I can't gauge how much,
How little.

I think in time—
Given the right depths,
Meanings,

Pin-pricks in himself—
He'll know that even the dead
Respond reproachfully.

space travellers

Fingers on the controls,
Star-points everywhere
Out there.
My second is command
Is stretching, waiting. We share

The same direction, plan—
Pierce a vacuum to find
God knows what exactly.
The air in here's just right
As we plunge toward a speck
After nowhere, peace.

Our children cry; their room
Is near and so we wake.
Lovers still we learn
Again—the place from which we left
Is where we now return.

II

in this street

1
normal

The street is normal
although a neighbour right-hooked
his wife last week and
that old midget next door
wheeling his barrow of rubbish up
to the dump
could not hold his water

and leaked against my
savage, picket fence. 'Piss off!'
I screamed, high up my
ladder. There's a sabre-
toothed tiger waiting to destroy its
politeness—
deep down, I think, in me.

Strange: I was told a
friend rose quickly from his chair
on Sunday and waved
to all his pets, children
and his wife. He left his TV set—
walked, dissolved,
right through a feature wall.

2

the house next door

Grass grows precisely
here; not one blade is taller
than others. This house
is for the use of reason,
but the family
was terrified (once
only) when they sat eating
at six o'clock in
the garden. On one
green, stately evening they saw
a sunflower change,
blur—grow hard again—become
a skull on a stem.
This was bleak enough,
and yet what really chilled them
was the easy way
the stranger simply
joined in the conversation
and snapped at insects.

postman

One day I'll steal the postman's bike—
After filling a bag with letters,
Poems from poets asking for publication—
And willy-willy down the street to where he lives,
Blow a whistle and dump the bag.
Then in a tree outside his window
I'll watch him read them one by one
Until the postman's head explodes, reveals
A frenzied garden, vultures
And party balloons released and leaving this world.

funeral

It's cruel, predictable
And worse than black.
                      Eyes
Have more than usual moisture—
Some of which is grief
Not dust, a summer wind.

You look into your skull—
An old habit easily done
In public—and then recall
How, one day, sitting
Near your mother's coffin
You saw in nearby shadows
Your mother floating like silk
And trying to speak.

being demolished

Intense and carrying speed
The freeway in twelve months
Will go right through that living room
And over the river.

A life is carpets and chairs
Piled up in the backyard,
And they make a bonfire
For children and dogs.

```
        d
bull  o      w           r
      z        a      e
        e    l    v
        r    l    o
```

Destruction ends
With a baptism of dust.

When I topple illusions
They reassemble, brick by brick.

revolution

for Evan Jones

1

night of the révolution

Neighbours tell of neighbours dying—
But nothing certain. For me walls are certain
And light that abdicates the floor.
I live gravely with rumours,
Unease, the nights, the gnawing
That could be rats up in the ceiling.

I drink a little, read a little,
And music worries from the wireless.
'Revolutions aren't like this,'
I tell my glass. Cats fight on a fence
Against a reddened cloud outside my room—
Their sound the only sound to blood the sky.

In bed at midnight I dream of yachts
Taken by air, determined,
Then revolutionaries, wrecked and drowned,
With faces negative like shadowed sand.
At dawn I wake not knowing violence,
Though far-off violence has tacked my life.

2
the new regime.

Trucks deplete the city,
Gear lives to executions;
Then bodies are burnt.
Day after day reactionaries
Go by—enclosed, unseen
Because the crowd might pity,

Question, label death extreme.
I smoke and watch, wonder
If my thoughts are crimes—
Think my thoughts are read
By the provost at the corner. . .
Go over what I've said.

'The New Regime must kill,'
I'm told. I've lost my faith in it.
Against my shadows, my room,
Revolt for me is still the same
Articulation as the frail
Persistence of a candle-flame.

3
years after

I see myself after the coup of twenty years ago,
Remember light encouraging the lean, new leaves.
My name is filed by the State,
But the worst order is my old age.

Like coral seen beneath the sea,
My days, my years, have left their minute skeletons
As firm as abstract monuments
That tell of public days of terror and colour.

protest

With arguments and slogans
We march up to a wall
And waiting policemen.
Windows,
High above our protest, open—
And so the evening goes.

Few people notice clearly
A man
Pummelled near a tree:
A girl, held by her feet,
Ends clawing in a van
That blades two headlights down the street.

I find myself in a mob
That hardly knows its cause—
My right place, I think.
I hear someone was killed.
Surely murder has won
When every shade of martyrdom is done.

the patriarchs

The gutters are advertising blood—
Trickles only, but growing.
I'm tired, tired of death

And yet the fathers are convincing; they say
They're killing train-loads for the common good,
Or merely axing evil patriarchs.

a modern leader

The name, wide on banners:
The face, governed by shadows,
Can't be defined.
He's all we have—
The nearest silhouette to God.

Radicals at night
March placards through the streets;
Not meaning murder
They are murdered
When he stamps their names.

The timing's poor. Enraged,
People act with lights,
Stripping the leader of shadows
To show him merely plastic
Melting, damning passion.

Voices, back-room powers,
Preach loudly from a wall
To mollify the people:
'He was a fool—be quiet—
Death is soon repaired.'

It's done like miracles
For even as we stare
A new and plastic leader
Rises, forms and darkens
Before a crowd that wants him.

Mr. Noah

The summer storm peeled iron from a roof
And plucked the palm trees. Debris drowned three cars.

We saw it coming—flood of manic clouds—
But never thought this afternoon would be a vortex.

In sudden rain and wind order unhinged
Briefly: children cried, a woman tore her dress,

But one old man, who'd built an Ark,
Sailed toward clear sky with all his animals.

Crowhurst

Crowhurst's damaged boat was found in the mid-
Atlantic 8½ months after he set out from the
resort town of Teignmouth on the southern coast
of England. Crowhurst, 36, was missing.

—from a newspaper report, 1969

Alone at sea,
Sailing the world alone
In a trimaran,
Crowhurst writes in his diary,
'The dead men gave a groan.'

'Others in this race
Around the world must lose. Others!'
Crowhurst withers to a grin
And radios false messages,
Positions out. His mind grows thin,

Eaten by salt.
'The bloody boat is being eaten!
All my fault.'
England hears four words—'I'm in the Pacific'—
Buoyant, unbeaten.

Lies: he has to lie.
He hasn't left the Atlantic. Lies,
For who'd believe Crowhurst
Is playing chess for his life
That pitches to nothing like seagull cries?

an eighteenth century gentleman
plans a portrait

I'll employ a painter
To freeze my family, myself
Triumphant before mountains:
A moment but not a moment
Because it can't have breath,
Only patterns serving gestures.

I'll stare right at the foreigners
Walking a bland, new century
Admiring the texture of smiles.
A painter's arabesques
Are his rhetoric
To go with colour and nonsense.

The arguments, the bed
My wife has never seen,
That my mistress knows, are real:
But when that century looks,
And my mind is earth,
Truth will be a painting.

Lies can't emerge through paint
To creep on varnish;
And that's the way I aim each day—
Deceiving yet never showing
Deception to those who love my life. . .
More a painting than I want to say.

the iconoclast

a citizen of Constantinople — 726 A.D.

I'm told—here's Christ. I can't accept
That circle where my gaze begins
A journey down the regimented stones.
I almost hate Christ against their golden void.

The pagan gods are dead but linger,
Looking from His tessellated face.
He should transcend mosaic, be in my head—
And so I put Him there to reign those walls.

Yet even as I live the face, the eyes,
The holy facets give themselves to stone again.
I'm trapped by walls, a church, the ultimates
Of ice and fire. My Lord in me is dead.

two deaths

1
potter

Working at the wheel he usually talked:
I listened. Those hands were dominant.
Conversation easily went
Beyond the attributes of clay and hands
Even on that afternoon
He understood his sickness.

Lying in hospital—morphine taken away
During the terminal hours—
His eyes were little more than water.
He needed death, not pity,
As I watched the hand of a potter continuously
Spidering back and forth over the blanket.

2
father

Ninety-one, in hospital,
He drinks a bottle of port
Daily. The nurses disapprove
And yet accept each bottle
Like a final right. He can't take living
Hardly able to move.

Brittle, honey-combed,
His spine gave out.
His daughter, over fifty now,
Is diligent and tries to bring him back
To speech, inventions, sunlight.
She's just a cow

Like the other cows who come
To wash a desert of flesh. He doesn't care
After a bottle's done—it gives a sense
Of death, what death might be:
A limpid drift away from silly healing.
My child is dense.

She's really just a child.
Daddy! Daddy! Get up. It's late.
And so he rises into air that's free
Of drugs and embrocations,
Becomes the ceiling
Looking at his body.

actions

1
springtime

He planted a realm of seeds
Neatly and with pessimism
That goes with a lack of green fingers.

He merely read the packet, hoped
He understood, believed each plant would struggle.
'So much for parenthood,' he told himself.
'The world's turning.'

2

Antarctica

After his talking destroyed her
He looked down at the rocks below. . .
The sea filling a cave, the way it retreated.

Left on that summer cliff above the breakers
He lifted his head to glimpse far off
A miracle—Antarctica
(Or so it seemed)—
A white, a glass thread
Incredibly expanding.

And then he knew he knew himself, grew cold.

the gift

The gift comes in a courtly box.

She holds it in her hands awhile.
Reconciliation made by the box
Will last, she says. Though tense with style,

The knot unclenches, and curling back
Lets the paper release the box:
Days are dead that once were black.

What troubles her, removing the lid,
Is many inhuman days in a box,
Time wasted, moments that have slid

Aside like paper wanting string.
The future, too, will be a box
Yet it will expand and never bring

Presents of regret, or cast
Her idly away like string and a box—
It will show her ways to wrap the past

Away, and ways to live in a box.

III

Hardiman's progress

for Bill Walker

If one doubts the necessity for controls,
reflect on this statement: it has been
conclusively demonstrated by hundreds
of experiments that the beating of tom-
toms will restore the sun after an eclipse.

E. Bright Wilson Jnr., in an
American scientific journal

1

Hardiman smoking

(scene: Stonehenge)

My name is Hardiman
And though it tells of strength
Ten minutes turn to ash
Too easily. My whims,
Concerns will go in a flash.

Don't let my name deceive;
I'm not stone in a field,
Yet I've learnt to endure
Landscapes in myself
For which there's little cure.

But I've seen in myself—
Primal, blank, alone
Like blades of stone in the sun—
The jubilant, the proud,
That last and won't be done.

2

the interview

(scene: Melbourne)

The pen doesn't abate;
The interviewer plots my life,
Although it's late.
Windows outside tell life
Until the blinds like guillotines
Efface the people talking and eating
Beyond administrations and routines.
A shock!
        A question comes;
Then grave and dull the face returns
To facing paper, tea and crumbs.
Outside a dome burns
And dims, and resurrects itself,
Edged with light. Despite my words
The interviewer writes his words,
And I regard the dead on a shelf,
Tombed and alphabetical.
Leaving I'm aware
Of cells packed tightly
Through necessity,
And how my days add up
Like patchwork.
              Night locks the town.
I choose with care
Ways to put chaos down.

3

a latter-day Canute

Waking from the nightmare
Of drowning deep in money,
I'm glad my room is the same;
Nothing has changed its name,
Or taken the hungers.

I lie awake and worry
About my debts—my bladder nagging me,
Depleting thought and actions—
And find, like moments in a dream,
I spend my life confronting oceans.

4

tightrope walker

Somehow I live by balance,
Not daring extremes.
I pussy-foot on a rope,
Judging, hoping, weighing
Above a chasm.

The tightrope was a game
When parents taught me
To venture from their platform.
The altitude I find
Gives a view to giddy and sway.

I have a skill:
Rope sags beyond the lights,
Rules where I must go—
All else is suicide
Or accident.

So I determine a life
And life determines me.
With my arms stretched out
I try to envisage a man
Sustained without a tightrope.

5

lunch on the grass

Today it's easy to decide that birth
And death are equal voids of innocence,
While gardens are a period between
And let me doze.

Children play in sand near where I eat.
I read of progress till I feel men play
With pyramids like children building higher,
Causing failure.

I fear that if I live to seventy
I'll be as resolute as men in stone
On pedestals, who want my eyes, my thoughts
Till nothing's left.

I'll go down paths before old age triumphs
And makes me see life as a pyramid—
Or limpid desert, mad without the palest
Hope of hills.

6
sun-bather

The bay, a repose of light
With no demands on me,
Gives sense to a fleet of yachts.
Spread out I copy its breadth
And close a book that destroys
Old notions of the soul
As wavelets make their sandy noise.

I can't pin-point the soul.
As flesh begins to burn
The shadows are salvation.
Spread out I see I'm nothing
And know this with a joy
As true as a water skier's
Passing beyond a buoy.

Gramley Library
Salem Academy and College
Winston a , N.C 2/108